The Adventures of Eros and Psyche

Written by I. M. Richardson
Illustrated by Robert Baxter

Troll Associates

Library of Congress Cataloging in Publication Data

Richardson, I. M.
    The adventures of Eros and Psyche.

    Summary: Relates how Psyche fell in love with Eros,
the god of love, and became an immortal.
    1. Eros (Greek god)—Juvenile literature. 2. Psyche
(Greek deity)—Juvenile literature. [1. Psyche (Greek
deity) 2. Eros (Greek god) 3. Mythology, Greek]
I. Baxter, Robert, 1930-   ill. II. Title.
BL820.C65R52   1983   292'.211   82-16057
ISBN 0-89375-861-2
ISBN 0-89375-862-0 (pbk.)

Aphrodite looked down from Mount Olympus and anger flashed in her eyes. She was the goddess of love and she was worshiped throughout the world because of her great beauty. But what she saw now made her angry and jealous.

On the earth far below, Aphrodite saw a lovely princess. The princess had two sisters, but she was far more attractive than either of them. Her name was Psyche, and she was so beautiful that people came from near and far just to gaze upon her. Some even said she was more beautiful than the goddess of love.

In her jealousy, Aphrodite turned to her son, Eros, the handsome god of love. "Go down and shoot Psyche with one of your arrows," she said. "Make her fall in love with the ugliest monster in the world. That will teach her not to challenge my beauty." So Eros took his bow and his magic arrows and went down to earth.

Time passed, but Psyche did not fall in love. Her two sisters married, but Psyche remained at home. Handsome young men came to worship her, but they did not ask for her hand. Although she was more beautiful than anyone in the world, Psyche was very sad. People treated her like a goddess, instead of a person.

Finally, her father asked the advice of Apollo, the god of truth. Apollo told him, "Your daughter will be the bride of one who flies through the night like a winged serpent. His terrible power is feared even by Zeus himself." Then he added, "Take her to the top of the mountain, and leave her there. The wind will carry her away to her husband."

The next morning, Psyche and her sorrowful family climbed to the top of the mountain. It was more like a funeral procession than a wedding march. Then they left her at the edge of a cliff and went away. Suddenly, a gentle breeze lifted Psyche up off the mountain and carried her far away.

She was taken to a beautiful palace made of marble, silver, and gold. "This does not look like the home of a monster," she thought. Then she went inside, where she found a banquet table prepared for a wedding feast. Invisible servants began to wait on her. They told her that she was the mistress of the palace and that everything in it was hers.

That night, she met her new husband for the first time. She did not actually see him, because the entire palace was in darkness. But he was kind and soft-spoken, and she soon fell in love with him. "Everything you want shall always be yours," he said. "But if you ever try to see my face, we will have to part. Then you shall live in misery."

One night, her husband said, "Your sisters are at the top of the mountain, weeping for you. But do not speak with them, for they can only bring us trouble." Psyche replied, "I am alone every day, and I am not permitted to look upon your face. At least let my sisters come here for a visit." At last, he agreed. "But do not tell them that you have never seen me," he warned.

The next day, the wind lifted the sisters up off the cliff and set them down before the beautiful palace. They looked with envy at the riches that surrounded their sister. They wondered who her mysterious husband could be. "He is young and fair-haired," said Psyche, "and he loves to go hunting in the mountains."

As the day passed, the sisters grew more and more jealous.
"Why should all this wealth belong only to our sister instead
of to us?" they whispered. A little later, without thinking,
Psyche said that her husband was dark-haired. Now her sisters
knew that she was lying. "You have never even seen him
yourself!" they cried.

"Have you forgotten what Apollo said?" they cried. "Surely your husband is a terrible monster who plans to kill you." Now Psyche began to fear for her life. "Wait until tonight," suggested her sisters. "Then, while your husband is sleeping, light a lamp and steal a look at him. If he is a hideous creature, you have no choice but to kill him." Then they handed her a long, sharp knife.

That night, Psyche waited until her husband was sleeping soundly. Then she took the knife from beneath her pillow and crept out of bed. She lit an oil lamp and turned to gaze upon her husband's face. What she saw startled her so much that she dropped the knife to the floor!

Before her was Eros, the handsome god of love! Instead of making Psyche fall in love with an ugly monster, Eros had secretly taken her for his own bride. Now a drop of hot oil fell from the lamp and landed on his shoulder. He awakened and said, "Where there is no trust, there is no room for love." Without another word, he arose and left the palace.

Psyche hung her head in shame. "What have I done?" she cried. "The god of love was my husband, and because I did not trust him, I lost him!" Then she vowed to prove her love for him. "Perhaps if I spend my life searching for him," she said, "I can someday win him back."

Meanwhile, Eros returned to Mount Olympus. As soon as Aphrodite learned what had happened, she became more angry and jealous than before. She vowed to find Psyche and make her suffer. Then, without a word, she left the home of the gods and went down to earth.

18

When she saw Psyche, Aphrodite began to laugh. "Your beauty has already begun to fade," she said. "If you want to keep a husband, you must learn to serve him—and I will be glad to teach you." Then she dumped a great pile of tiny seeds on the ground. "Separate them!" she commanded. "And make certain you finish before I return." Then she turned and went back to Mount Olympus.

Psyche looked at the pile of seeds and began to cry. "My task is hopeless," she sobbed. "It would take me a hundred years to separate all these seeds." But an ant heard her, and soon an entire colony of ants scurried back and forth, placing the seeds in separate piles. When Aphrodite returned, she flew into a rage. "Your next chore will not be so easy!" she promised.

"Fetch me some golden wool from the sheep that live by the river," she commanded. Psyche knew of these terrible sheep. They lived in a thicket of thorn bushes, and were so fierce that no one dared to go near them. As she approached the sheep, Psyche heard a voice saying, "Wait until evening. Then, when the sheep leave the thicket, you can take the wool that has stuck to the thorns." So that is what Psyche did.

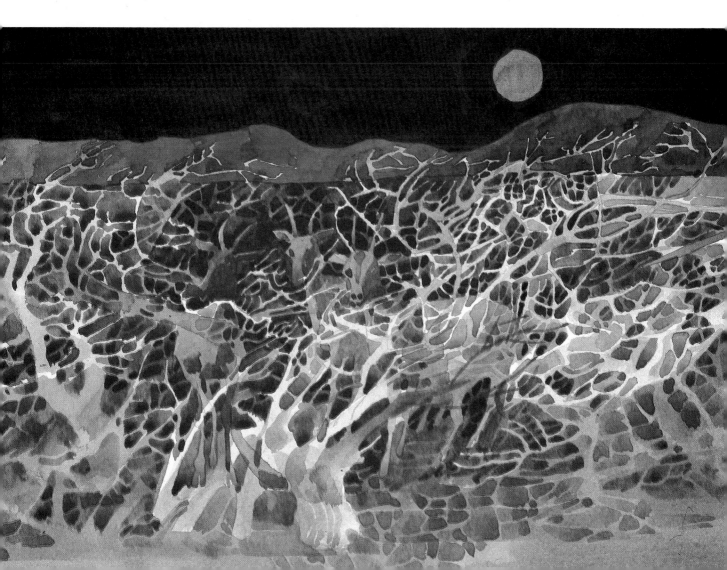

Next, Psyche had to fill a jar with water from the top of a
dangerous waterfall. The rocks nearby were so slippery and
jagged that no one could have climbed them. Psyche sat down
and began to weep. Suddenly, a great eagle swooped down
and seized the jar. He flew up and filled it with water from the
very top of the waterfall, then set it down gently at Psyche's
feet.

When Aphrodite saw that the jar had been filled, she only glared at Psyche. Then she ordered her to perform an impossible errand. "Go down into the lower world," she said. "Find Persephone, the Queen of the Dead, and ask her to fill this box with some of her immortal beauty. Then bring it back to me at once."

Psyche thought she would have to be dead before she could get into the lower world. So she vowed to kill herself by jumping from the top of a tall tower. Suddenly, she heard a voice saying, "If you ever wish to return to the world of the living, there is only one way to get into the kingdom of the dead." Then the voice told her what she must do.

She did exactly as she was instructed. She took two barley cakes with her, and she put two coins into her mouth. Then she went to a foul-smelling cave that was the back entrance to the lower world. Inside, a dark tunnel led deep down into the depths of the earth. Even as she started down, Psyche knew it would be a long and dangerous journey.

After she had traveled a good distance, she came to an old man and a lame donkey. The donkey was pulling a cart that was overloaded with sticks, and the sticks kept falling off. The old man asked Psyche to help him pick up the sticks, but she did not answer him. The voice in the tower had told her that this would be a trap set by Aphrodite. So Psyche passed on by.

26

She kept walking deeper into the earth, until she finally reached the river Styx—the boundary of the lower world. There was only one way to get across, and that was by bribing Charon, the ferryman of the dead. As soon as Charon had taken one of the coins out of Psyche's mouth, he allowed her to get into his leaky ferry.

Even when she had reached the other side of the river, Psyche could not rest. Now she had to get past Cerberus, the three-headed watchdog, standing guard at the gate of the kingdom of the dead. But Psyche gave him one of the barley cakes she had brought with her, and he allowed her to pass through the gates unharmed.

At last, she stood before the Queen of the Dead and explained why she had come. Persephone put something into the tiny box and immediately gave it back to her guest. Then Psyche began her long journey home. She used the second barley cake to pass once more through the gates. And she used the second coin to get back to the other side of the river Styx.

When she had finally come out of the foul-smelling cave, Psyche foolishly opened the box. Instead of immortal beauty, an invisible death-like sleep came out and swept over her. But Eros came to her rescue. He wiped the sleep from her eyes and locked it away. Then he told his wife to deliver the box to Aphrodite without further delay.

As soon as Eros had returned to Mount Olympus, Zeus called the other gods and goddesses together. "It is time for Eros to stop wandering about the world," he said. "He should settle down here on Mount Olympus. Unfortunately, the wife he has chosen is a mortal, who cannot set foot in the home of the gods. Therefore, I have decided to grant her immortality."

Then Zeus sent Hermes, the messenger god, to bring Psyche up to the home of the gods. A huge celebration followed, at which she drank from the cup of immortality. Now everything was suddenly changed. Since Psyche was no longer a mortal, Aphrodite had no reason to be jealous of her. The goddess of love gave her blessing to Psyche. And at last, Eros and Psyche were together again.

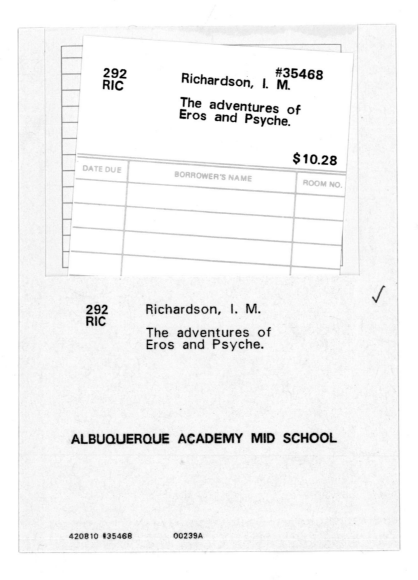

292
RIC

Richardson, I. M. #35468

The adventures of
Eros and Psyche.

$10.28

DATE DUE	BORROWER'S NAME	ROOM NO.

292
RIC

Richardson, I. M.

The adventures of
Eros and Psyche.

ALBUQUERQUE ACADEMY MID SCHOOL

420810 #35468   00239A